The Little Lass and The Sailor

By

Sara Bell

ARose Books
Incline Village, NV / Allison Park, PA

BOOK AND COVER DESIGN BY MARCELLA PARSONS

COVER IMAGE: *ARRIVE DANS LE PORT BY LAFFTTE*

ISBN 978-0-9846081-1-9

Rose Books

AROSE BOOKS
INCLINE VILLAGE, NV / ALLISON PARK, PA
WWW.AROSEBOOKS.COM

Arrivée Dans Le Port by Lafitte

The Little Lass
and
The Sailor

By

Sara Bell

The Little Lass and the Sailor

Once upon a time,
Not long ago
There was a little lass
Whose hair was red aglow

The lass worked hard by day
At all that she should do
Went merrily to tasks
On dreams that no one knew

One day she met a man
Smiling bold and cocky
A handsome man was he
A sailor from the sea

The man stood some above her
As strong as he was bold
And spoke that he would court her
And treat her as of gold

His blue eyes flashed upon her
From warm and weathered skin
His hair a wavy black
With grey bespeckled in

The Little Lass and the Sailor

The lass felt shy and pretty
By such a swarthy fellow
He talked of ships and sailing
Of sky and wind and sea
He spoke of far off places
Not word of which was mellow

The lass went on to town
The sailor on her mind
On her face the telltale
Of the glow he left behind

Her friends who waved in passing
Stopped to question her demeanor
She told them of the sailor
And of his wish to see her
But ah, yes they knew him
So they told her so
A man of many tales
Of which she ought to know

They spoke of sea adventures
Of women and of wine
They told of brawling battles
And the hardness of his mind

The Little Lass and the Sailor

They said that he would hurt her
Such a tiny lass was she
They said she shouldn't see him
Just let him go to sea

The lass heard all and pondered
The stories she was told
She conjured up his vision
And matched it sure and bold

She couldn't reconcile them
With what she saw and knew
Of the mighty sailor
Whose spirit seemed so true

When he came to find her
The little red-haired lass
She knew she would go with him
Whatever came to pass

He led her to his ship
Of which she had been warned
She thought of all the stories
Then looked into his eyes
She slipped her hand into his
And felt that they were lies

The Little Lass and the Sailor

The ship loomed large above them
Upon the glistening sea
The sun in casting shadows
Bode fearful mystery
He led her up the plank
And held her tiny hand
He displayed before her treasures
From many a far land

He sat her on a chair
Of silk and soft spun gold
Her feet upon a stool
Mahogany so old

Then the handsome sailor
Of treasures he did choose
Some silver at her throat
Some beautiful blue shoes

For hours they did talk
Upon the rolling sea
He told her of adventures
Of places she must see

The Little Lass and the Sailor

The little lass she listened
For so she loved his tales
She watched his eyes aglowing
Flashing stormy gales

The lass told of her life
So simple by compare
He'd put her in his pocket
Take her everywhere

To distant lands of mountains
Jungles and the sea
To dance and sing with natives
To laugh and to be free

When they stopped their talking
She felt there was no end
They were on a journey
That had only to begin

The lass felt as a feather
Blowing on the wind
The sailor strong and proud
Was surely taken in

The Little Lass and the Sailor

When once they reached her land
With warm and smiling eyes
The sailor took her hand
And swore he told no lies

He promised to return
From sailing on the sea
He said his blood would churn
By her side he must soon be

But to sea he must now go
For it was in his soul
Although it did not show
Resistance took its toll

So, on and on the people chattered
Of the lass and sailor
They talked of this and talked of that
As if it really mattered

She told them of his gentle hands
As if she would just break
She told them of his kindly words
That soothed her heart's soft ache

The Little Lass and the Sailor

They questioned her as to his plans
Was she treated badly
She told them all to no avail
Of which she noticed sadly

So many nights they sailed together
Standing side by side
Their laughter heard like waving heather
Blown in with the tide

One day the sailor left his lass
To visit his first child
Many days and nights had passed
For the son lived in the wild

His son that he would visit
Such a proud and handsome man
Now had a wife with baby
All living off the land

The sailor went to find them
To see how they would fare
To see if he could help them
With the new life they would bear

The Little Lass and the Sailor

The sailor found his kin
In a grove within a forest
Surrounded by the din
Of creatures not at rest

He found the life they started
Not so strong you see
Within the day departed
In Heaven it must be

His children lost and harried
So in their nest they stayed
And soon the babe he buried
A prayerful tuned he played

The sailor did not stay long
There was nothing more to say
He left to make his journey
The sea in just one day

A great and mighty sadness
Stole upon this man
A man of many tales
Many far off lands

The Little Lass and the Sailor

He could not bear the thought
Of the tiny baby's fate
It tore inside his soul
And greatly slowed his gate

He thought of other tragedies
Which all gained heavy weight
A long and woeful list
Chalked on a heavy slate

And even his two loves
Could not now set him free
The little red-haired lass
And sailing on the sea

He veered off from his trek
And headed for a wood
Where lived an evil witch
In nothing was she good

She had a fearsome brew
Said to stop the mind
From sorrowful thoughts
Or feelings of like kind

The Little Lass and the Sailor

He gave her coins of gold
To purchase this fierce brew
And drank it as she told
His soul to be made new

His mind was eased his heart was soothed
His spirit leapt on fire
The seaward trek now so much smoothed
Life was not so dire

He must now hear gulls harsh jeers!
He must seek dangerous lands
To conquer all his hidden fears
The witches brew in hand

What of the little red-haired lass
And of their joyous love?
A fragile thing of broken glass
With the baby gone above

The little lass she watched for him
And saw him take his ship
She saw him with the witches brew
Strapped upon his hip

The Little Lass and the Sailor

She saw him toss his head back
A fierce laugh he just then made
She heard his fist — a mighty crack
On weathered balustrade

And off he sailed on glittering sea
His hair blown in the wind
On rolling waves of majesty
A sea without an end

The lass came everyday
To scan the sea's horizon
To search for her sailor
And the ship that he did ride in

But all that was seen
Was the ebb and flow of tide
The endless waves that stretched
Out to his dear sweet side

One day she stopped her looking
And headed north by west
To find a lovely meadow
Was the object of her quest

The Little Lass and the Sailor

A lazy winding stream
With trees along the shore
A place of dreamy visions
Of stories and folklore

It was here that she first met him
The man encased in light
With flowing hair and beard
And robes of brilliant white

He came while she did rest
Beside the quiet stream
And spoke to her in peaceful tones
As if it were a dream

He laid out many paths
Winding through her life
Showed her which to follow
Which would cause her strife

She came to trust his guidance
To know that He was true
To know that she must seek Him
In all that she would do

The Little Lass and the Sailor

Beside the quiet stream
She laid her pretty head
And waited for the Master
On her flower bed

Not long did she now wait
To see Him cased in light
Again she was quite struck
By His gentleness and might

No word need pass between them
For the Master knew it all
He knew of her sweet sailor
And the fate he must befall

With sadness in His heart
And tears within His eyes
He told her she must leave him
And bear her painful sighs

He said she could not follow
Along her lover's road
Her grief she must now swallow
Her own journey she must bode

The Little Lass and the Sailor

Again He gave her courage
Though all her dreams were gone
Somehow she could continue
With hope, life would move on

She knew she could now bear
Her life as it had been
Hard work and prayer and quiet
Had some peace for her within

Her sailor she would love
And dream of him at night
She'd miss his eyes and laughter
His arms so full of might

She knew that she was lucky
To know him as no other
To know his true great spirit
And not his worldly cover

With love she did release him
To his rolling sea
To his witches brew
And whatever he must be

The Little Lass and the Sailor

And what of her handsome sailor
Out upon the sea
His pain and anger drive him
Without rest or sweet company

On sea he fights the pirates
With fists and knives and guns
He fights them for their plunder
And his anger not undone

On land he heads for taverns
Of dim and smokey veil
And passes on his witches brew
To others who do sail

They drink and laugh and curse
Throw fists with mirth and glee
And conjure up grand stories
Of sailing on the sea

When he sees the women
Bejeweled and dancing round
He thinks of his sweet lass
And drinks another round

The Little Lass and the Sailor

Then on and on he sails
Over rolling sea
To fight the endless battles
And laugh with mirthless glee

Great storms he must sail through
Though mast and sail are shorn
Great battles he must fight
Though muscle and limb are torn

Great drafts of brew he drinks
Though he wishes not
Great sadness he won't feel
Of lost love and battles fought

The Master knows the sailor
And the pain he can not own
Patiently He waits
For the sailor to sail home

www.ingramcontent.com/pod-product-compliance
Lightning Source LLC
Chambersburg PA
CBHW031618040426
42452CB00006B/589